MW00606583
LIFE
Science
For Visual Learners
BY
VIDYA SUDARSAN
SARAH JANE EDWARD-SEBENI
SCIENCE VISUALLY SERIES

First Edition - August 2016
Paperback ISBN: 978-0-9979419-0-6
Library of Congress Control Number: 2016913159

Published by EdVisually, Inc. D.B.A. EdVisually Books
Send all inquiries about special discounts on bulk purchase, or for any other information to: EdVisually, Inc. 39270 Paseo Padre Pkwy PO Box #433, Fremont, CA 94539 USA
www.edvisually.com

Printed in the United States of America

Dedication

To our daughters, Maya, Amita, Kesiena, Tejiri and Tega.
For motivating and inspiring us with their love for Science.
And to all children who love to learn visually.

Acknowledgments

We want to thank our husbands, parents, extended family, and friends for all their tireless support and encouragement without whom this book would not have come to fruition.

TABLE OF CONTENTS

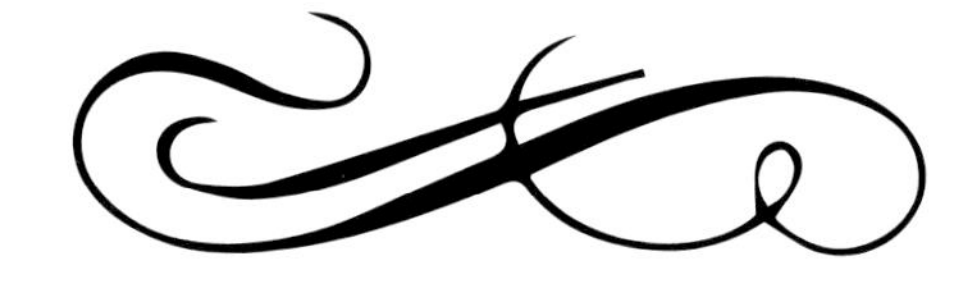

FOREWORD

Children are magical. They have a natural sense of curiosity and are uniquely capable of learning. Traditionally, the learning process relies heavily on language, both printed text and verbal discourse. When a child struggles with language, parents and educators often make assumptions about a child's limited capacity to learn, especially concepts that are scientific and conceptual. When appropriate tools and supports are available and used, the opportunity for learning unfolds for that child in ways that are unprecedented.

EdVisually's concept beautifully supports the unique learning needs of children who struggle with language and learning. The progression of this book follows a path that is accessible to a child's natural learning process. The scientific concepts in this book start with the child making connections to things she already knows and experiences that are already familiar. Each subsequent chapter uses this same approach, heavily relying on clear photographs of real objects, to introduce and reinforce concepts covered. When you, along with your child or your students, work through the book together, discussing the concepts and making real life application, the magic of learning will be made real.

Jennifer Adams Oppenheimer, MA, CCC-SLP
Founder, SpeakJoy Center for Development

INTRODUCTION

Background History: How This Book Came About...

Once upon a time, there was a beautiful baby girl. She came into this world with special needs and was on the autism spectrum. Like all children, this little girl had the curiosity, zeal and enthusiasm to learn about anything and everything around her. As she grew, her mother realized that there were limited resources available to teach her daughter certain subjects, particularly science and social studies, which she loved. Her mother discovered that the tools accessible to her were not suitable for her eager learner since her beautiful daughter was a highly visual learner. This beautiful girl soon began to make significant and rapid progress in learning about the world around her as her mother placed real life images in front of her in a sequential flow. Hence, the dawn of a new way of visually learning science through images.

Synopsis: Who Will Benefit From EdVisually Books...

The goal and purpose of this book is to support diverse learners in the classroom. EdVisually aims to use its teaching materials primarily as a visual learning tool that services a range of students with differential learning styles and needs. It provides a scaffolding method framework for educators and parents to help and support learners to visually understand academic subject matter and concepts by making important cognitive connections with them. Factual knowledge about science concepts as well as other academic subject matter is presented predominantly through the use of numerous real life photos rather than solely by text. Learners will benefit most when this content is paired with interactive oral instruction. Mainstream classrooms can also benefit from this book as an added reinforcement tool. All EdVisually books are presented primarily using real life visual images. Fun trivia, entertaining illustrations, and interactive questions further break up the texts, making it easily accessible and engaging, while promoting active learning. The implementation of the scope and sequence of the Science Visually series is left to the discretion of the educator, as they see fit, and/or according to the needs of the learner(s). Now, let the journey begin...

Sarah Jane Edward-Sebeni

Chapter 1: Living and Nonliving Things

Our planet is made up of living and nonliving things. Plants, animals, and people are all **living things**. Another word for a living thing is an organism. An **organism** is any independent living thing. It can be as small as a single celled bacteria, or as large as a whale.

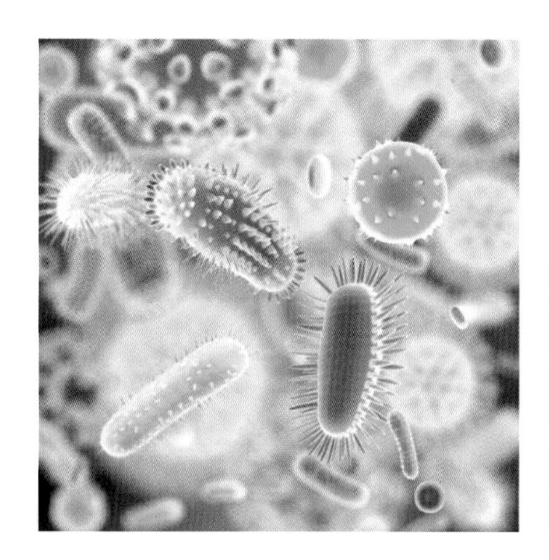

Organisms breathe, grow, move, and reproduce. **They need air, water, and energy to live**. They also respond to changes in their environment and **adapt** accordingly to it. For example, flowers wilt under the hot sun and shrivel in the cold snow. This is similar to how we put on a jacket when we get cold, or put on shorts when we feel hot as a response to where we are.

Organisms are made up of **cells**. Cells are the building blocks of life. Anything that is alive is made up of many, many cells. Did you know that there are 37.2 trillion cells in one human being? This means that there are many cells inside of you and me. Each cell carries out all of the jobs needed for survival. Without cells, no living thing would be able to do all the things that it is able to do.

Organisms take and use energy from their surroundings. When you eat your favorite snack or lunch, do you ever wonder why you have to eat? This is because **food** gives you **energy**. Energy is what helps you do a lot of things necessary for life. You need energy to move, run around, and play. You need energy and nutrients to help you grow tall and strong.

All living things live where they can meet their needs. To survive in an environment, they have to **adapt** accordingly. For example, humans cannot live underwater and a redwood tree cannot grow in a desert.

All living things reproduce. If a living thing didn't **reproduce**, then it would go extinct or not exist anymore. That is why humans make babies. The ways living things look and behave like their parents are known as **traits**. That is why we look like our parents.

As we have learned so far, living things have special qualities that make them different from non living things. **Nonliving things**, on the other hand, do not exhibit any characteristics of life. They **cannot breathe, grow, move, reproduce,** or **adapt**. Rocks, sand, and dead animals lack this ability completely.

Both dead things and objects that were never alive make up the category of **nonliving things**. Furniture, clothing, shoes, musical instruments, toys, books, and vehicles are some more examples of nonliving things.

SCHOOL BUS

If you look outside, you will find many rocks. Pick up a rock and put it to your ear. Can you hear it breathe? Do you think it needs air, food, water, or energy to live? Will this rock grow bigger? No. Rocks stay the same and do not grow. They also can neither move on their own, nor reproduce. So, is this rock a living thing?

Name 4 living things and 4 nonliving things that you see around you. What are the differences?

Living Things	Nonliving Things
1.	1.
2.	2.
3.	3.
4.	4.

What is the difference?

Living Things	Nonliving Things

Now, do you want to know more about living things like plants, animals and people? Let's first take a closer look and learn about plants.

Chapter 2: Plants - Producers

Plants are living things. From the tiniest flowering plant called the watermeal to the giant sequoia tree, plants come in all colors, shapes, and sizes. More importantly, plants are not only rich in color and variety, they are central to life on Earth. They can grow and produce food. They can also provide many non-edible products for other living things to use. Everything animals and humans eat comes directly or indirectly from plants. Plants provide vitamins and minerals that are required nutrients for all living things.

Plants not only produce food, but they also produce oxygen in exchange for the carbon dioxide in the air. This process cleans the air, and we get oxygen to breathe. Plants also cool down the air by absorbing the sun's heat and blocking sunlight. Unlike animals, plants are rooted in place. They cannot move around on their own from place to place like animals. The only way plants can move is if they are moved by a person, an animal, or by the wind.

Did you know? Some plants, called meat-eating plants, get extra food from eating insects and other tiny animals. One such plant is called the Venus Flytrap. It has moving parts that catch their prey.

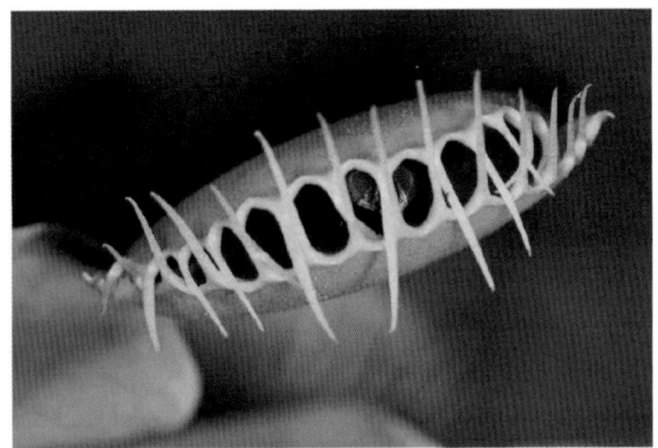

Parts of A Plant

A plant has many parts. It is made up of roots, a stem, leaves, seeds, flowers, and fruits.

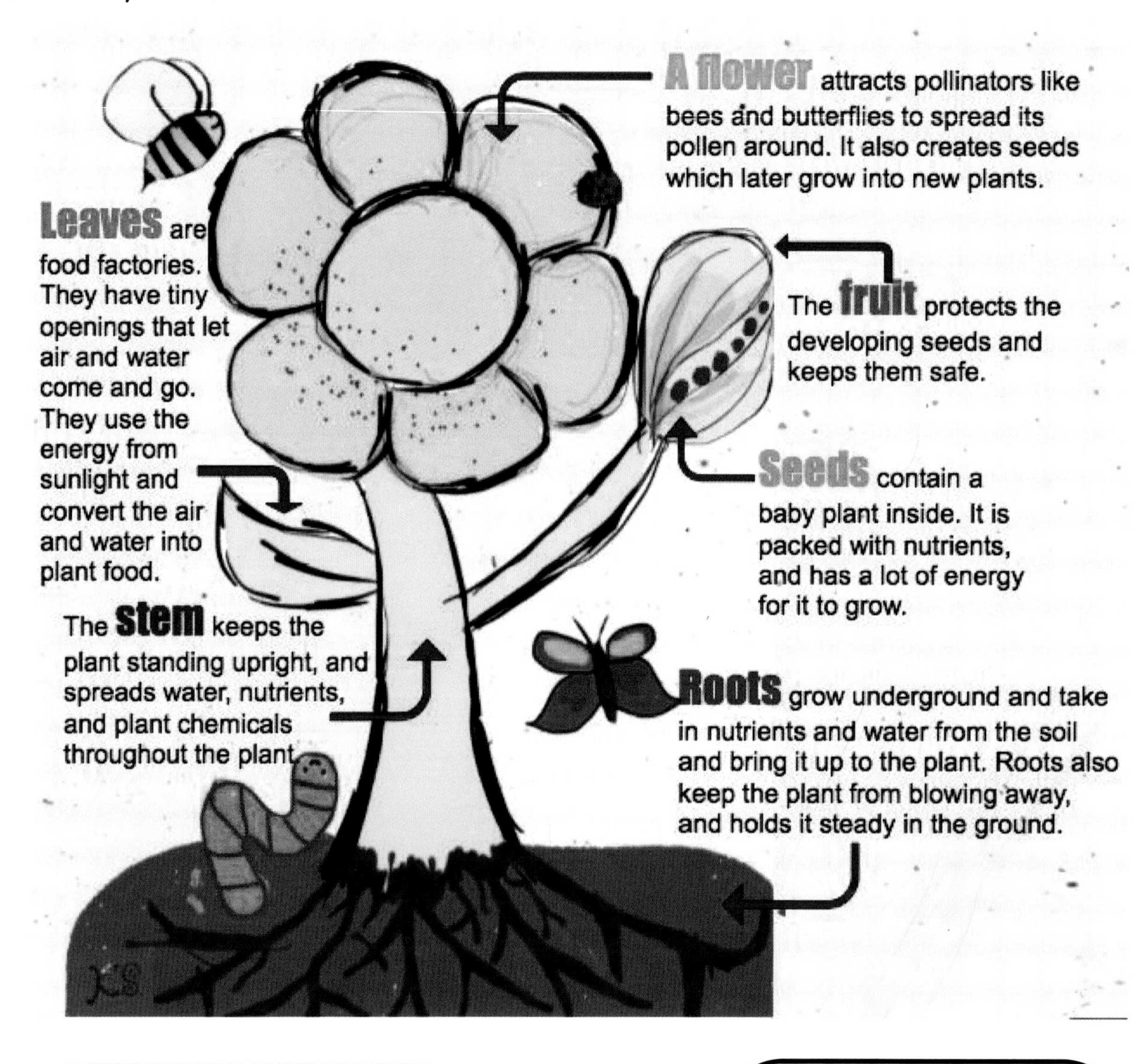

Did you know? Just like a straw is used to suck up a drink, plants have straw like tubes called xylem inside their stems to do the same and suck up water from the ground.

What Do Plants Give Us?

Plants give us many important things that help us and our environment. Plants make the **oxygen** we depend on to breathe. They also produce all kinds of **fruits**, **vegetables**, and **seeds** for us to eat. They even provide material like cotton that our clothes are made of. First, let's look at fruits!

Fruits are fleshy parts of a plant that are delicious to eat and that are very nutritious for your body. **Only plants that have flowers can make fruits.** They contain seeds and can be juicy or crispy, sweet or sour, and smooth or fibrous. Fruits can usually be eaten straight from the plant without any cooking.

Name one of your favorite fruits. Describe how it looks and tastes.

Did you know? The strawberry is the only fruit that bears its seeds on the outside.

Flowers produce seeds. They grow on a stalk, are usually colorful, and are surrounded by petals. Flowers have many enticing fragrances and nectar that attract bees, hummingbirds, and other animals. These birds and animals move the powder inside the flowers, called **pollen**, from one flower to another so that other flowers can create seeds. This process is called **pollination,** and without this, there would be no new plants.

Name three types of flowers. Describe how they look and smell.

Plants produce **vegetables** that we eat everyday. Unlike fruits, different vegetables are produced in different parts of the plants. The vegetables we eat may be **roots like carrots**, **stems like celery**, **leaves like spinach**, and **flowers like cauliflower**.

Have you been to the produce section of a supermarket or grocery store? Describe what you see.

> Did you know? A tomato is actually a fruit, not a vegetable.

Now, let's explore the different types of vegetables plants produce for us to enjoy.

Leafy Vegetables: Cilantro, Spinach, Cabbage, and Bok Choy

Stem Vegetables: Asparagus, Celery, Rhubarb, and Bamboo Shoot

Did you know? It takes the asparagus three years to grow from seed to harvest.

Root Vegetables: Beet, Onion, Carrots, and Ginger

Flower Vegetables: Artichokes, Broccoli, and Cauliflower

Did you know? The broccoli you eat is actually baby flowers that haven't bloomed yet. It tastes bitter once the flowers open.

Pod Vegetables: Okra, Green Peas, and Edamame

Name and describe five types of vegetables you know.
What is your favorite vegetable? Describe how it looks and tastes.

Now, let's explore the other types of food that plants produce for us to enjoy. **Nuts, seeds,** and **grains** are other edible foods that plants produce.

Nuts: *Almonds, Cashew nuts,* and *Pistachios*

Seeds and Grains: Sunflower Seeds, Quinoa, and White Rice

Did you know? Rice has been feeding us for 5,000 years. The first known account was in China about 2800 BC.

Spices are another contribution that plants make for us to use. A spice can be a seed, fruit, root, bark, berry, flower bud, or other vegetable substance primarily used for **flavoring, seasoning, coloring,** or **preserving food**. Pepper is a fruit, clove is a flower bud, and cinnamon comes from the bark of the cinnamon tree.

Spices: Pepper, Cinnamon Sticks, Cloves, and Cardamom

Name some of the spices that your family uses in their cooking.

Did you know? Earth has more than 80,000 species of edible plants.

Isn't it amazing to learn about all the different types of foods plants can give us?

What are some of your favorite dishes? Can you name some of the vegetables that are in it?

There are also a lot of other types of products that we use that also come from trees. Let's take a look at some of these.

Wood Products come from trees that are larger plants with very long and huge stems called trunks, which support the branches and leaves. A lot of things come from wood. In fact, paper, the material that this book is made of, comes from trees. The trunks of trees also produce wood that we use to build our homes and furniture.

List five types of wood products you see in your home.

Apart from providing us wood and paper products, there are many other things that trees also produce for us to use and enjoy. **Rubber**, **natural resin**, and **maple syrup** are just a few products that can be obtained through the process of tapping certain tree saps, which is the fluid found inside tree trunks. Many everyday products such as tires and gloves can be made from rubber, and plastics, paint, and medicine can be made from natural resin.

Tree Saps: Rubber, Natural Resin, and Maple Syrup

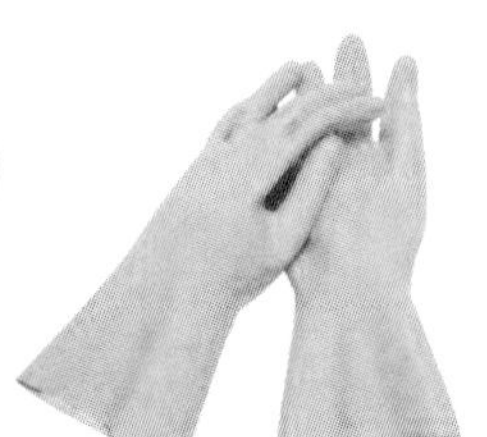

Did you know? Over 5000 products are made from trees.

Cotton is another very important product that plants give us. It is a soft, white, fibrous substance that surround the seeds of the cotton plant, and is used as thread for sewing and making all kinds of fabrics.

Name five things around you that come from plants.

Other ways that larger plants, in particular, trees, are useful to us, is the **shade** they give us on a hot, sunny day.

They also provide homes in their trunks and branches for many birds, insects, and animals.

Did you know? Koala bears spend up to 20 hours a day sleeping or resting in trees. They curl up around tree limbs and grip them with their feet.

Types of Plants

Now that we have learned about what plants give us, it's time to learn about the different types of plants and how they look. Based on their height and how they grow, **plants can be grasses, shrubs, vines, and trees**. There are also categories of plants that can be of the flowering and non-flowering variety. This means that some plants have flowers while others do not.

Grasses are a type of plant that can be very short in height like the one found on a soccer field. It can also be long like the one you see on the hills. The world's most significant food source comes from grass. Pasture grasses provide food for farm animals like cows, sheep, and goats. Some grasses are used for human consumption such as wheat, oats, and barley. Wheat is used to make flour, which is the most important ingredient in a birthday cake, or your favorite bread. Oats are used to make a popular breakfast cereal called oatmeal.

Grain Producing Grasses: Rice, Wheat, and Oats

Short and Tall Grasses: Meadows, Park, Lawn, and Soccer Field

Animals Grazing on Different Types of Grasses

Did you know?
Bamboo is a grass.
It is the fastest growing woody plant in the world, and it can grow up to 35 inches in a single day.

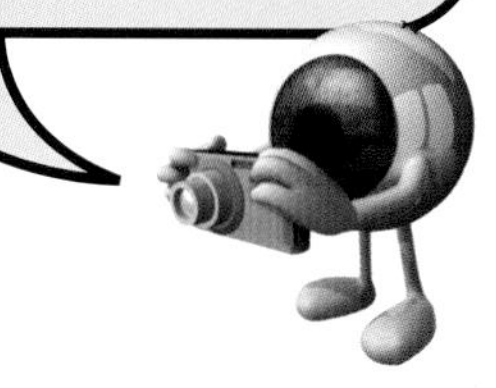

Let's go outside to a place that has grass. How does it look and feel when you touch it?

Did you know? Corn belongs to the grass family. It is a large grain plant which grows in "ears", each of which is covered in rows of kernels.

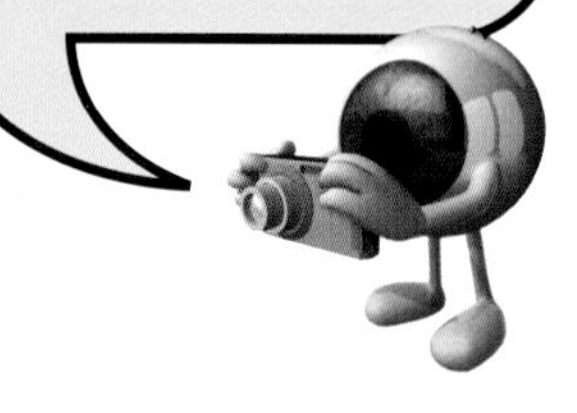

Animals Resting on Different Types of Grasses

Shrubs are small to medium-sized woody plants that are also known as bushes. They are different from trees as they are usually shorter in height and have many stems. These stems grow from the bottom up, and are usually of the same thickness. They are different from a tree, which usually has one fat trunk with many small branches. Most shrubs are smaller than trees and less than 20 feet tall.

Did you know? Blackberries are a type of tasty fruit that grows on shrubs.

Shrubs: Evergreen, Blueberries, Hydrangea, and Flaming Leaves

Do you see any shrubs outside your window? What do they look like?

Vines are plants that cannot support themselves, but grow long. They creep along the ground like melons, cling to a wall like an ivy, or are supported on wood sticks like a grapevine.

What makes vines different from shrubs? Describe this difference.

Did you know? Lianas are a type of climbing vine found throughout tropical rainforests. They have thick, woody stems and are used to make a variety of products like baskets, ropes and wicker furniture.

Water Plants, or aquatic plants, are plants that grow and stay in water all the time. Most of them grow in freshwater, not salt water. Some grow on the water surface and float, and some grow at the bottom of a pond. Water plants are different from other plants because they do not need to have roots that go into the ground. An example of a well-known aquatic plant is a water lily. Water lilies are circular, leaf-like plants that float on the surface of ponds, and sometimes they grow pretty white or pink flowers.

Let's go to a pond and look for some water plants. How do they look?

> Did you know? The Victoria plant, also called the giant water lily, is one of the biggest water plants on earth. It has a leaf that can grow to over 10 feet wide, all of it floating on water.

Trees can live for a very long time, some even reaching several thousand years old. Most trees have green leaves until it is the fall season. When fall comes, the leaves of some trees change colors. The leaves change into beautiful hues of red, yellow, and orange and fall to the ground. There are a few exceptions to these traits. Evergreen trees stay green all the time, even in the fall and winter. Also, some trees have leaves that are never green, like cherry trees which are actually purple and red.

Did you know? Trees grow from the top and not from the bottom.

Very Tall and Special Trees

Did you know? Trees breathe in what we breathe out. They pull in all the carbon dioxide out of the air and give us back oxygen. That's a real gift from trees!

Did you know? The bristlecone pine is the oldest tree in the world. It is about 4,845 years old and is found in the White Mountains of California.

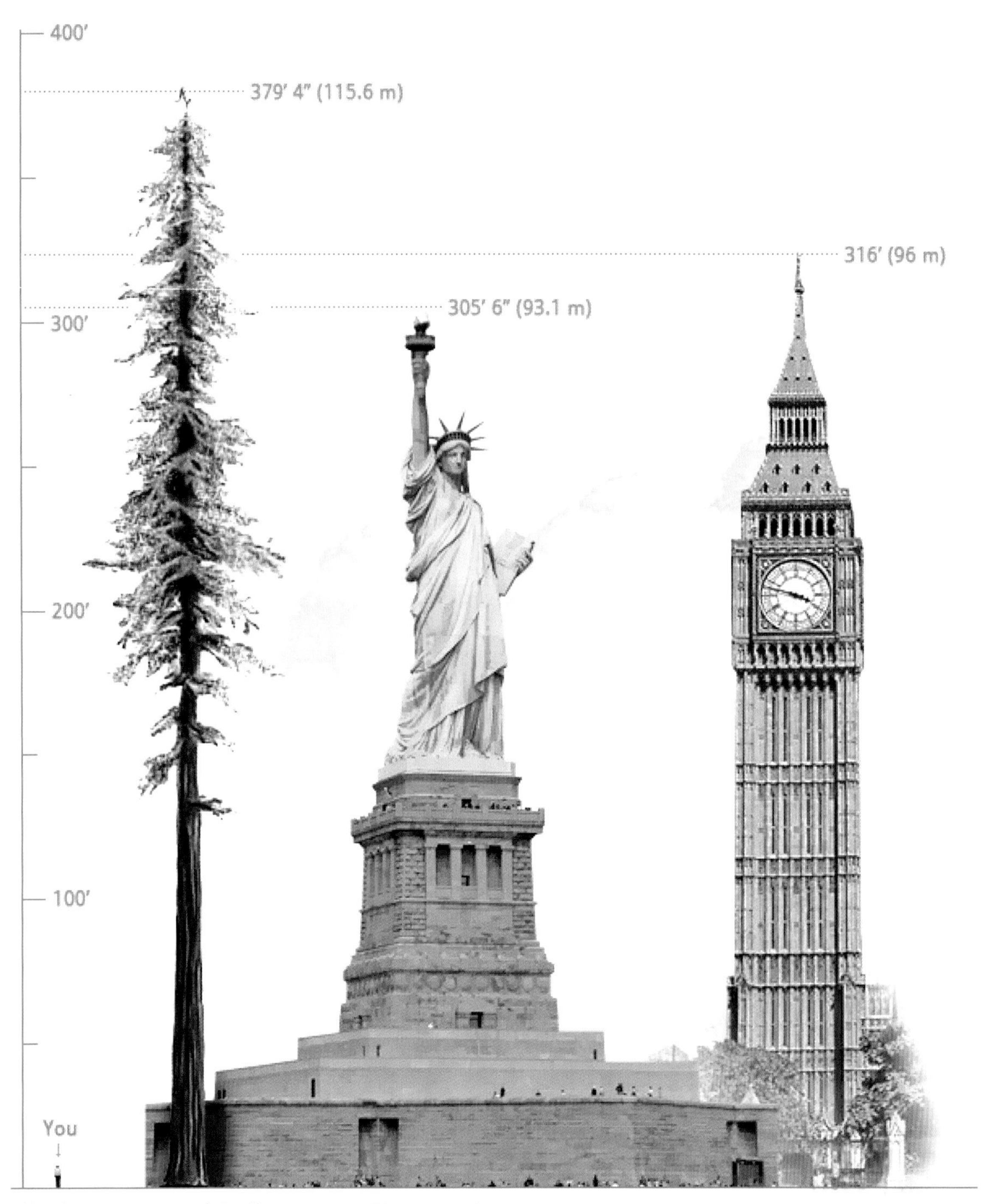

Height comparison of the Hyperion tree (iltwmt.com)

Did you know? The Giant Sequoias in the Redwood Forest of California are around 300 feet tall and weigh close to 3000 tons!

What is your favorite tree? Describe how it looks.

Are there any special trees in your neighborhood? What are they?

Flowering Plants are plants that can produce flowers. Nearly ninety percent of all plants bear a wide variety of flowers. All flowers have very unique and diverse characteristics and belong to one of about 450 flowering plant families. Some of the most important and diverse ones are the daisy, orchid, and grass families.

Count how many flowering plants there are in your neighborhood?

Non-Flowering Plants are plants that do not produce flowers. Pine trees, firs, cypresses, junipers, cedars, and redwoods are some types of non-flowering plants that use seeds, while ferns and mosses use spores.

Spores are very small and light, and they are moved from one place to another by wind. They can be moved to new locations where they can grow. There is also another group of non-flowering plants called the fungi, that include mushrooms, and these also reproduce by spores.

Did you know? Scientists estimate that some species of ferns have been around for over 350 million years.

How Do Plants Survive?

Plants need some very important elements to survive. These are water, sunlight, air, nutrients, the right temperature, and room to grow.

Have you ever wondered how a cactus plant survives in a desert? Under its thick, prickly skin, are soft tissues that absorb water like a sponge. When it rains, it takes in as much water as it can for storage for future use. It also grows very rapidly during this time.

Did you know? Plants that don't die off each season are called perennials. They keep making new seeds each spring and summer. Some examples include trees, daisies, strawberries, and foliage.

Did you know? The seeds from some plants need to be gathered and used to grow new plants each year. These plants are called annuals. Some examples of annuals are green peas, Zinnias, and wheat.

How Do Plants Grow?

Plants grow from seeds, and they also make their own seeds. A seed contains everything needed to produce a new plant. When a seed is planted in the soil and is given water, it starts to grow new plants. New plants have the same qualities of the parent plant. For example, a sunflower seed will grow a sunflower plant.

Roots then take hold of the soil and keep the plant in place.

Now the plant starts producing its own food using the process of photosynthesis, which is explained on the next page. Using this food, and the help of **water** and **sunlight**, it grows its stem, roots, leaves, fruits, and its other parts.

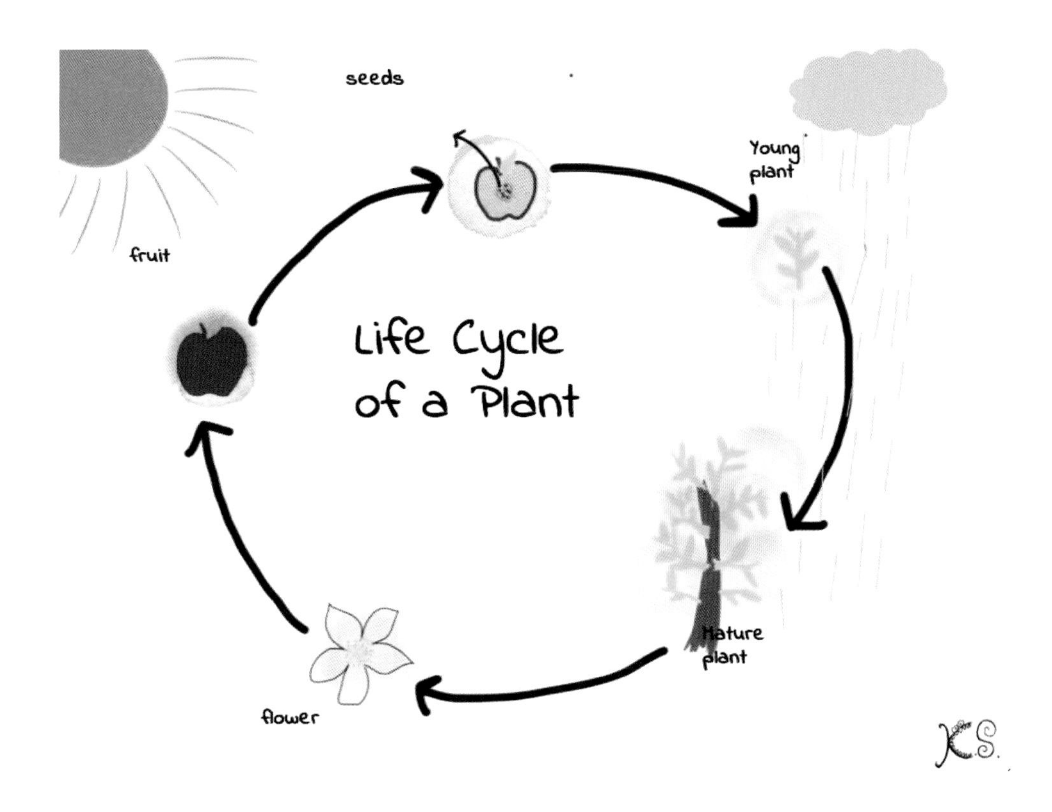

What are the two most important things a plant needs to grow?

Why did this plant wilt?

How Do Plants Make Their Own Food?

Plants are amazing because they make their own food. To grow from a sapling into a full plant, they first take in water and nutrients from the soil to their leaves, through veins which look like straws.

At the same time, small holes on their leaves absorb **carbon-dioxide** from the air. The carbon-dioxide and the nutrient-rich water mix along with a pigment on the leaves called **chlorophyll**.

Once **sunlight** reaches the leaves, the chlorophyll absorbs the sun's energy, and produces **oxygen** and the plant food called **glucose**. This glucose that is produced by this process is used to help plants grow roots, leaves, stem, seeds, fruits, flowers, and breathe. Without this glucose, plants cannot live. All the fruits and vegetables we love to eat come from this one substance. This process is called **photosynthesis**.

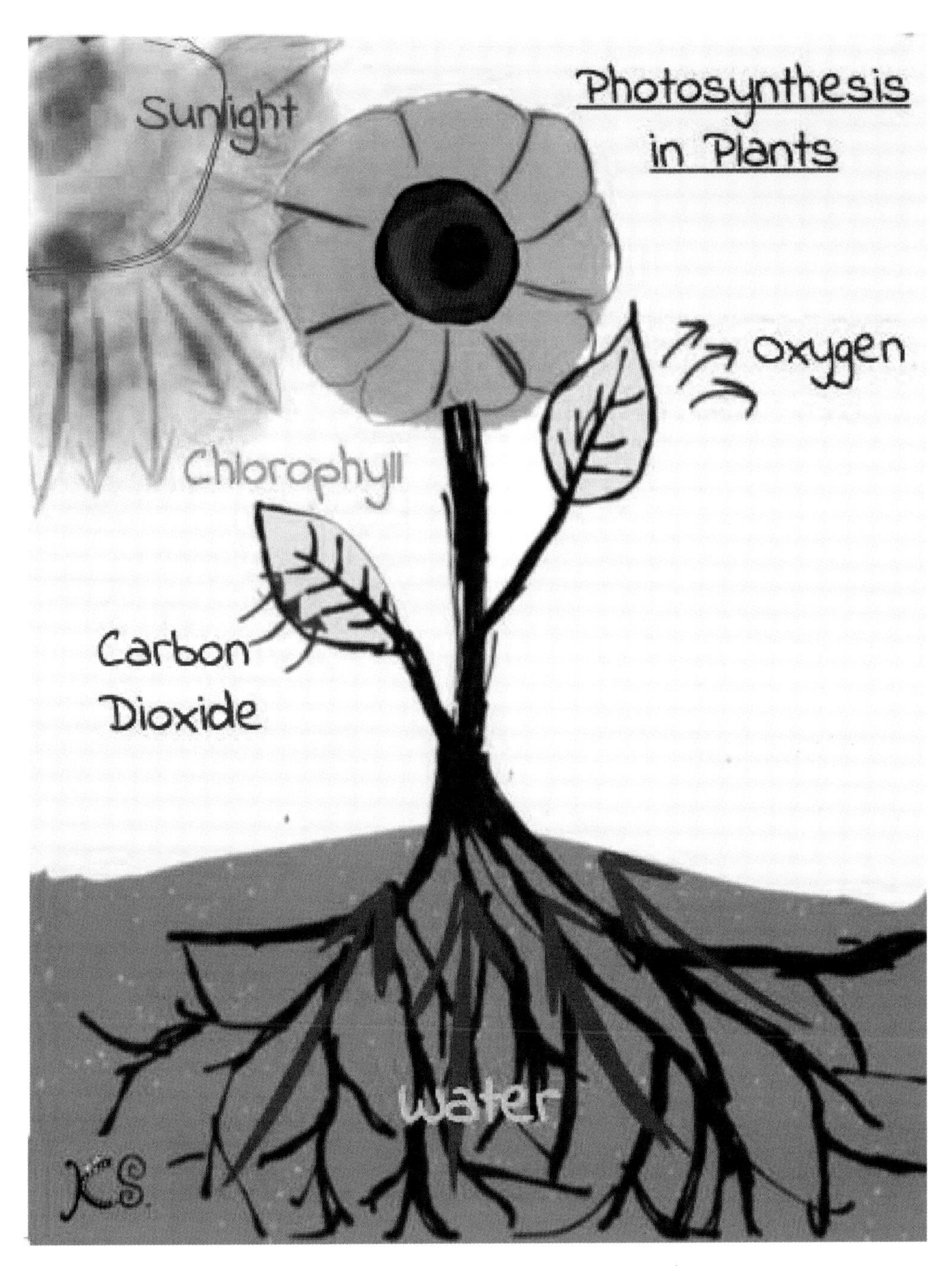

Why is sunlight so important for a plant to grow?

Did you know? Photosynthesis does not happen at night time because there is no sunlight.

Chapter 3: Animals - Consumers

Animals are also **living things**. They can **breathe**, **grow**, **move** independently, **reproduce**, **adapt**, and respond to their environment. Animals cannot produce their own food, but they survive by eating plants, and other animals. They get energy by digesting and absorbing the nutrients from the food they eat.

Sensory Organs

Animals have sensory organs that help them detect various things in their environment such as light, sound, smell, taste, touch, and temperature. They have varying reflexes that allow them to respond differently through these senses.

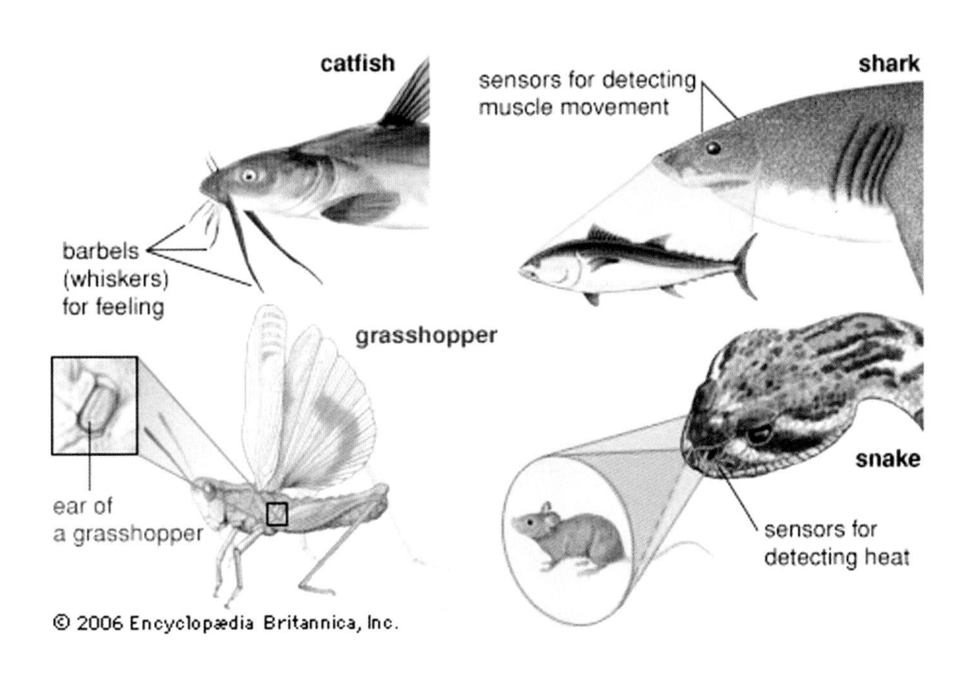

What are the five senses used for?

Skin Types

There are different types of skin or surface that is found on an animal's body. Some animals, such as the snail, turtle, and crab, have a hard shell on their bodies which protects their soft organs. Other animals have shiny, smooth, wet skin, like the frog, seal, and dolphin, to help them swim and stay in the water for long periods of time.

Some other animals have hundreds of scales on their skin, like the armadillo, or the alligator. Their scales are dry, rough, and sharp, and this helps them move, retain moisture, and defend themselves. Other skin types include feathers, fur, and hair, which keep them warm.

Invertebrates and Vertebrates

Animals can be separated into two main groups based on their inner body structure, namely **invertebrates** and **vertebrates**. The main difference between the two is that vertebrates have an internal skeleton, consisting of a backbone or spine with interconnected bones.

Invertebrates are animals without a backbone or spine. Insects, crabs, worms, and the octopus are some examples of invertebrates. They move by crawling, flying, or swimming.

Invertebrates

> **Did you know? Worms only use muscles to move because they don't have any bones.**

Vertebrates include fish, amphibians, reptiles, birds, mammals, primates, rodents, marsupials, and humans. While birds and fish fly or swim, most vertebrates such as lions, dogs, and humans, have limbs and can walk or run.

Vertebrates

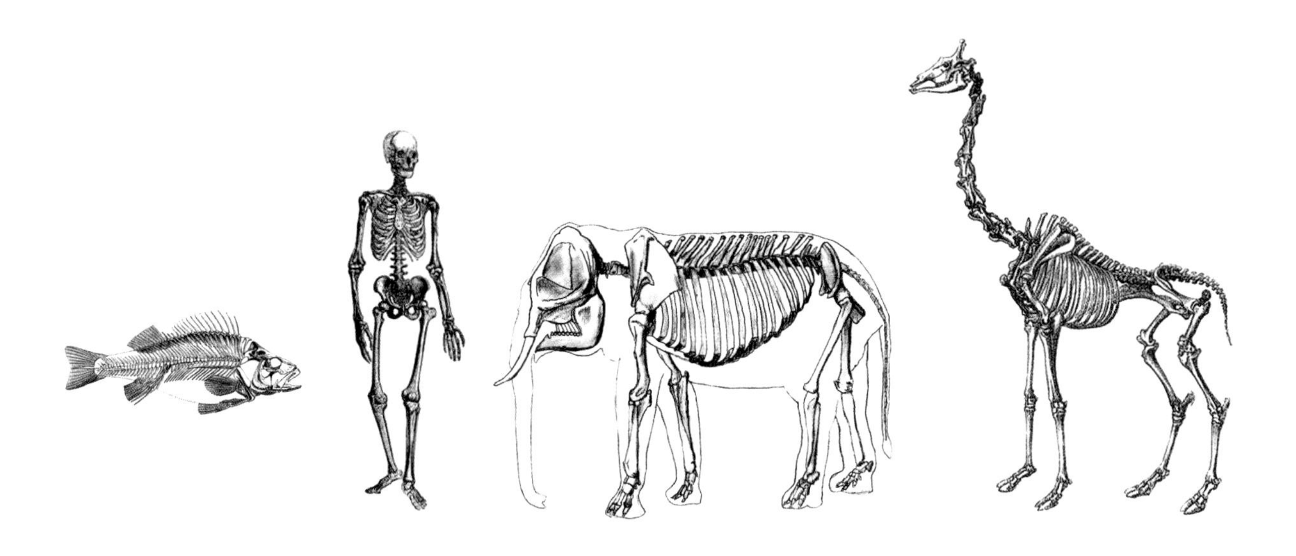

Can you guess what these skeletons are?

Warm and Cold Blooded Animals

Animals have sensory organs that are used to interact with their environment. These organs determine how they respond to temperature. An animal is either **warm-blooded** or **cold-blooded,** based on how they sense and react to the outside temperature.

Warm-blooded animals have bodies that stay at a constant temperature no matter the environment around them.

Warm-blooded Animals: Cats, Birds, and Humans

Cold-blooded animals become hotter or colder, depending on the temperature around them. They need the sun to warm them up, and the night, or water to cool them down.

Cold-blooded Animals: Dragonfly, Frogs, and Fish

Herbivores, Carnivores, and Omnivores

We can separate animals into groups based on their eating behavior. An **herbivore** is an animal that gets its energy from eating only plants. A **carnivore** gets its energy from eating only animals. An **omnivore** eats both plants and animals. Zebras and cows are herbivores. Lions and foxes are carnivores. Humans and bears are omnivores.

Herbivores: Elephant, Camel, and Goat

Carnivores: Tiger, Seal, and Fox

Omnivores: Human, Bear with Fish and Watermelon

Animal Classifications

We have learned so far about the different attributes that animals have. Now, we will take a closer look at all the various classifications into which animals can be grouped.

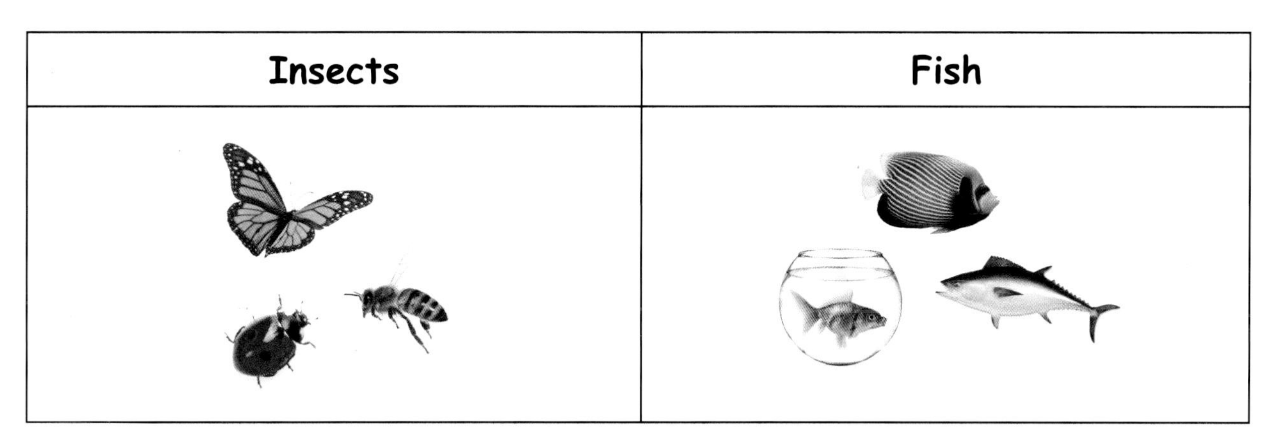

Amphibians

We can group animals based on a combination of how they breathe, where they live, and what they eat. **Frogs**, **toads**, **newts**, and **salamanders** are **amphibians**. There are around 6,000 different species of amphibians worldwide. They have been around for a very long time, and the earliest one to exist dates back to 368 million years ago.

Amphibians live both on land and in water. They have adapted to survive in many different types of habitats, but tend to live in moist places to keep their skin from drying out. They can be found in forests, meadows, rivers, lakes, ponds, swamps, and farmlands.

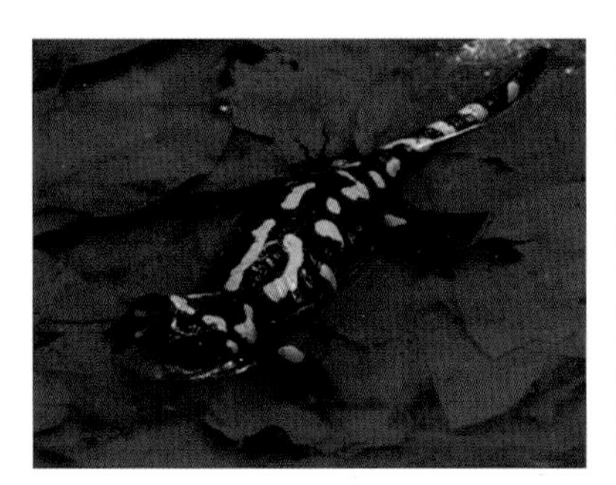

Amphibians are also cold-blooded animals and are vertebrates. They lay many eggs in the water, from which young ones hatch. To breathe underwater, amphibians have gills. Gills work just like lungs, but take oxygen out of water instead of air. On land, they can breathe through their skin and lungs.

Most amphibians can change the color and texture on their skin to mimic the environment. Their skin color can go from green to grey or brown within seconds. This behavior is called camouflage, and they use this to hide from predators.

Amphibians eat pest insects, slugs, worms, snails, and small fish. They usually hunt for food at night. Amphibians play an important role as living things. They eat insects like mosquitoes that spread diseases, and also, many animals like snakes depend on them as their food source. **Where can you find an amphibian?**

Did you know? Many amphibians have a long sticky tongue, which they use to catch their prey.

Did you know? When some frogs sing, a big bubble forms under their chin.

Reptiles

Alligators, turtles, lizards, and **snakes** are some examples of reptiles. There are around 10,000 different species of reptiles worldwide.

All reptiles live on land, except sea turtles, alligators, and sea snakes that live in water. They need to come to the surface of water to breathe. Reptiles prefer to live in warm and dry climates. They can be found on every continent except Antarctica.

Did you know? Sea turtles cannot breathe in water, but can hold air in their lungs for many hours.

Reptiles have scaly bodies and dry skin. Instead of ears, they have holes on the sides of their head. They are cold-blooded vertebrates, and lay eggs on land. Most baby reptiles are independant from the day they are born.

Did you know? Tuatara are rare, medium-sized lizards found only in New Zealand. They are the last survivors of an order of reptiles that thrived in the age of the dinosaurs.

While most reptiles eat other animals, some turtles and lizards also eat leafy vegetables.

Name as many different reptiles as you can. Which one is your favorite? Why?

Fish

Goldfish and **salmon** are a few examples of fish. There are around 30,000 different species of fish worldwide. Fish live underwater in oceans, rivers, lakes, ponds, and aquariums. They come in all forms, shapes and sizes. They can be colorful, small, short, long, or big.

They breathe using gills, which work just like lungs. However, they take oxygen out of water instead of air. All fish have scales on their bodies and have fins which protrude from their bodies. Fins are like legs. They need them to move under water. It helps them to keep stable, turn, and control speed while swimming.

Fish are cold-blooded animals. They are vertebrates with skeletons that are made of either bone or cartilage. Most fish lay eggs, but there are a few species that give birth to live young such as sharks. Fish eat plants that grow in water and also other fish.

Have you been to an aquarium? What is your favorite fish? Describe how it looks.

Did you know? Sharks can hear a fish 1600 feet away.

Did you know? Salmon can jump as high as 6.5 feet.

Insects

Butterflies, **spiders**, **caterpillars**, **ants**, and **ladybugs** are just a few examples of insects. There are around 950,000 different species of insects worldwide.

Insects have three main body parts, which are the head, thorax, and abdomen. The head has sensory organs. The antennae on the head of an insect help it "feel", sense temperature, humidity, and also smell. Insects that have wings can both fly and crawl.

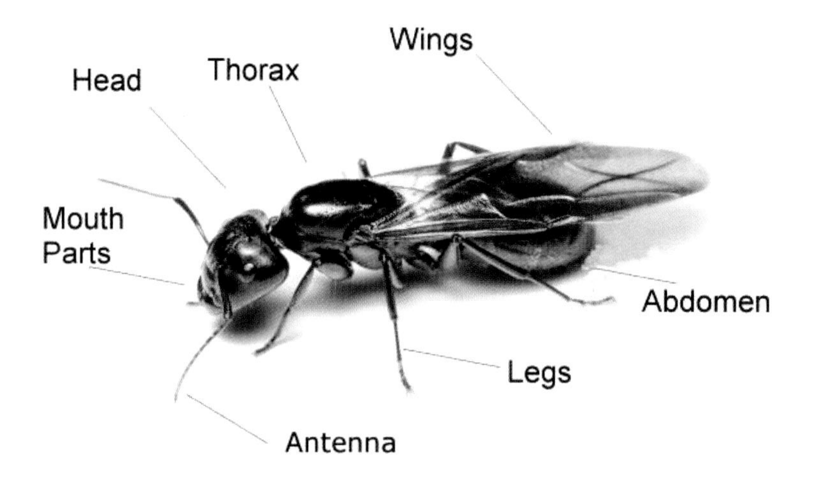

Insects are invertebrates and warm-blooded. They could be omnivores, herbivores, or carnivores.

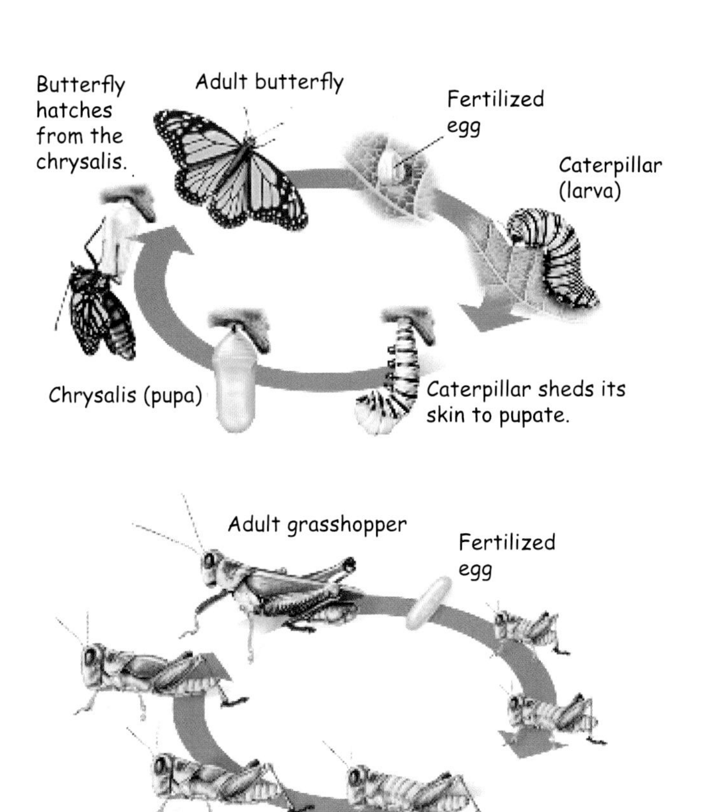

Did you know? The life cycle of a butterfly is different from a grasshopper.

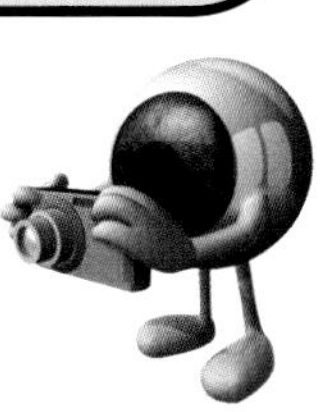

Did you know? Some insects,like ants and bees live together in colonies.

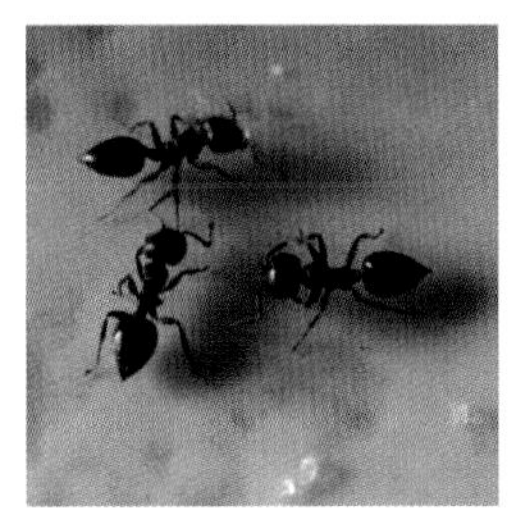
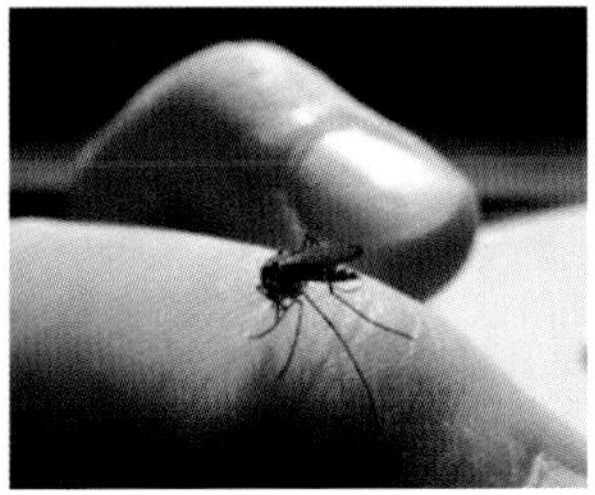

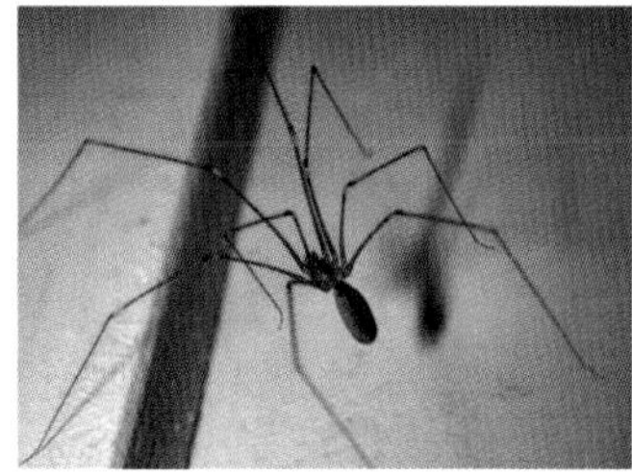

Honey bees, silkworms, ladybugs, butterflies, and many other insects play a vital role in the ecosystem. They make honey, silk, wax, and also help in plant reproduction. Insects also help clean the environment by breaking down garbage into tiny pieces.

What insects can you find around you? Are they big or small? How do they move? Do they fly, or only crawl on the ground?

Birds

Eagles, **peacocks**, **flamingoes**, **parrots**, **hummingbirds**, and **sparrows** are just a few examples of birds. There are around 10,000 different species of birds worldwide. Birds come in all sizes and can be very colorful. They have two wings covered with feathers that help them fly. They are also vertebrates and have hollow but strong bones.

Most birds can fly, and their bodies are very light. They are warm-blooded animals because they can generate body heat to keep themselves warm. Feathers also keep them warm.

Birds build nests where they lay eggs that hatch into chicks. They make their nests with twigs, leaves, mud, and feathers. Some birds use their saliva to hold a nest together.

Most birds are omnivores, but can also be either herbivores or carnivores only. They eat different parts of plants like fruits, seeds or nectar, and meats like worms, rodents, fish, small reptiles, other birds, and even large animals. A hummingbird eats nectar, and is considered a herbivore. A vulture is a carnivore, and eats only meat.

Did you know? Birds do not have teeth. Instead, they use their curved beaks to swallow their food whole. They will then break it into smaller pieces using their muscles.

What type of bird do you like? How does it look?

Mammals

Dogs, cats, lions, whales, and **humans** are a few examples of Mammals. There are around 5,500 different species of mammals worldwide.

Mammals are special types of animals where the females can give birth and feed their babies. They also produce milk using their mammary glands, and so they are called mammals.

Mammals are the only animals that have hair. Hair helps them keep warm and protect their bodies. They also have a diaphragm that divides their bodies into two parts. The top portion has the heart and lungs. The stomach and intestine are in the lower portion.

Mammals are warm-blooded vertebrates, and can be herbivores, carnivores, or omnivores. Carnivorous mammals have sharp teeth compared to herbivores. Most carnivores have eyes in front to spot their prey, and herbivores have their eyes on the sides to have wider vision to be able to notice a predator.

Did you know? Whales are mammals. They do not lay eggs. Instead, they give birth to babies just like bears and elephants.

What three mammals do you like? Why do you like them?

Humans

Men, **women**, and **children** are humans. They are the most intelligent of mammals. Humans, like other mammals, are warm-blooded, have hair, a backbone, and a diaphragm.

Humans are the only species to create culture, religion, and institutions such as family, marriage, education, and government.

Unlike animals, humans can communicate with one another using words to speak. They can use their brains to think and reason for themselves. They can also express what they are thinking or feeling by showing their emotions on their faces and with their bodies. For example, when we feel happy or sad, it can be seen on our faces. We can also move our bodies to play sports or dance to music.

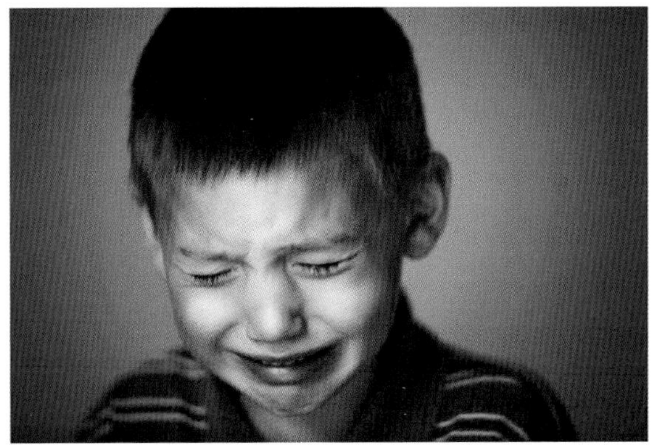

Humans are supremely intelligent. They have made books, invented all kinds of complicated machines, such as cars, computers, and satellites, and can solve complicated problems.

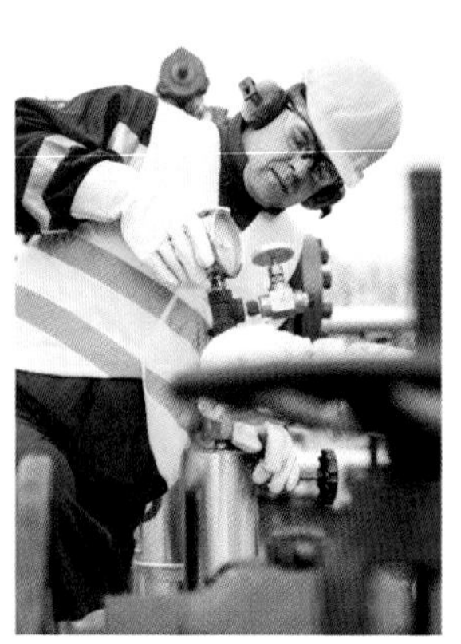

Name some other things that humans have invented.

Humans are good at remembering, calculating, imagining, and speaking. No other species has created language, literature, music, and art, or discovered mathematics or science like humans have. Some things humans can do that other species cannot do, are read, write, draw, paint, cook, and play musical instruments.

Humans choose to live together in families, and are very social animals. They make choices and decide how to live, where to live, and what they do everyday.

We have learned so much about animal classifications, their physical appearances, eating habits, and more. Now, let's take a closer look at where they can live.

Habitats

All animals need a place to live that provide them with food and shelter. Such a place is called a **habitat**. This place may be as large as an ocean or as small as a hole in your garden. The animals adapt to their habitat according to their needs. They have evolved their senses, and have adapted their bodies to survive with the limitations of their habitat.

Ocean Animals

The ocean habitat contains the greatest diversity of animals. This habitat includes the deep, cool and dark ocean beds to the warm open tidal surfaces of the ocean. Fish and water animals live in this habitat. These include deep-sea animals like the octopus, whale, and dolphin, to shallow water animals like small fish and jellyfish. This habitat also includes birds that eat fish.

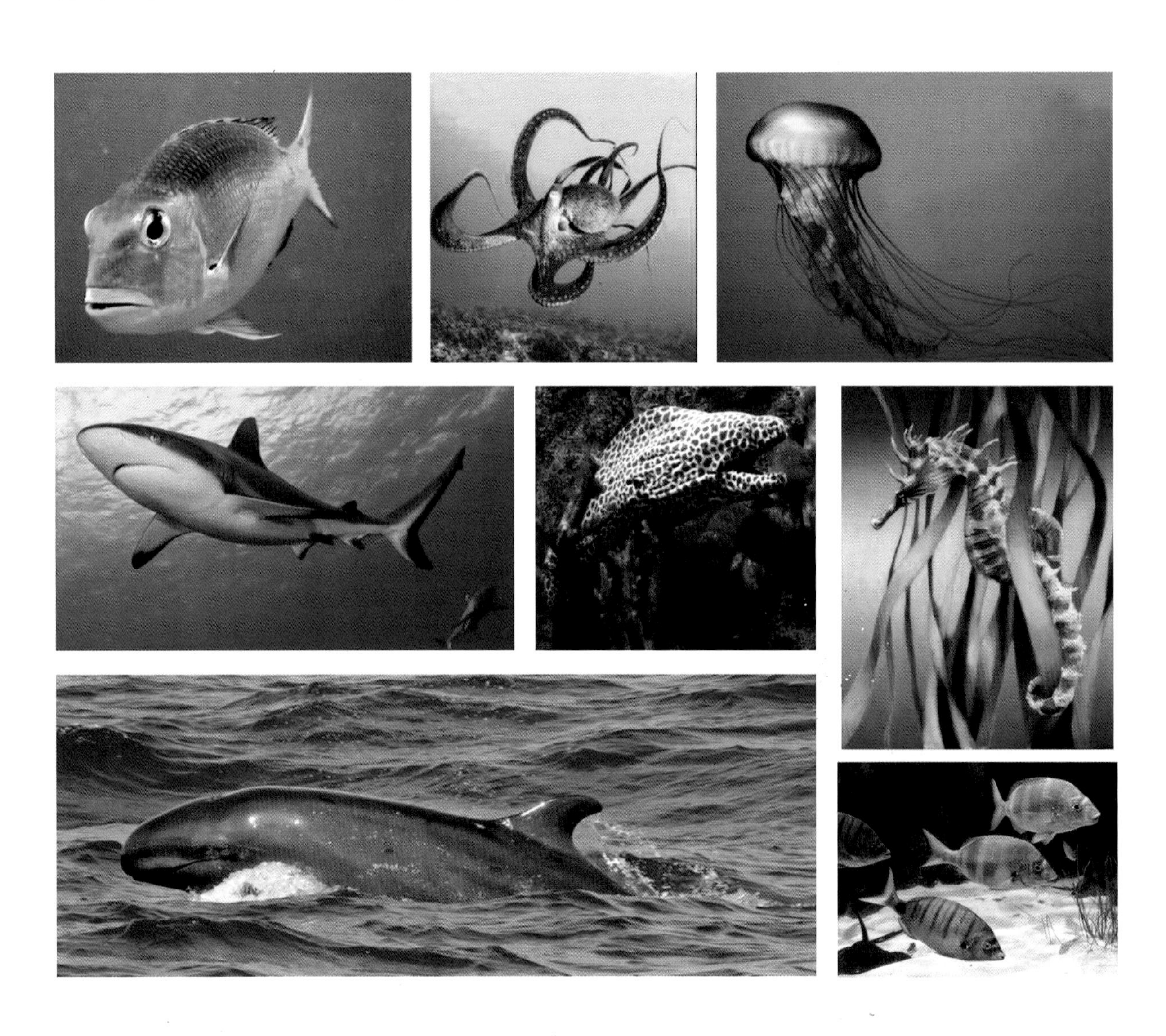

Which habitat contains the greatest diversity of animals?

Desert Animals

A desert is very dry, with little water, little vegetation, and has extreme temperatures going from quite cold in the nights to very hot in the days. Very few plants grow in the desert. An example of these plants is the cactus.

Animals, like camels, can store their own food and water to survive the harsh conditions of deserts. They can adapt to the extreme temperatures, and live in deserts for long periods of time. Reptiles are also suited to this habitat. They usually come out at night to avoid the harsh sun.

Did you know? Camels have large, widespread feet that help them walk in the hot desert sand without sinking.

Grassland Animals

The grasslands are a place that is covered with many grasses and grass-like plants that grow close to the ground. Rain is scarce, so trees cannot grow here. However, the vast amount of diverse grass helps keep the land warm and moist. It enables animals to live safely with enough food to eat.

Animals that live in this habitat include the lion, tiger, bison, giraffe, and elephant. Some animals graze on the grasses and some eat the grazing animals. Some of these animals live in large groups.

Did you know? The grasslands in Africa are called savannas.

Forest Animals

A place filled with dense vegetation from small shrubs to large trees is a forest. Temperatures range from humid, to wet, to cool.

Majority of the animals live in this habitat due to the abundance of plant food, water, and other animals. Animals make their homes in nests high up in the trees and burrows in the ground.

Why do forest animals like to live in this habitat?

Polar Animals

The land and seas around the North and South Poles of the earth are called polar habitats. These regions, are covered with snow or ice most of the year. The ground is too frozen for trees, so only short grasses and moss grow in this habitat.

Polar bears, arctic foxes, whales, and penguins live in this habitat. They have thick skin or thick fur to protect them from the cold, eat fish or other polar animals, and store food as fat on their bodies to survive the harsh winters. The animals live in holes in the ground or in ice caves. During the harsh winters, some animals, like the bears, hibernate, and other animals, like the whales, migrate south.

As we have seen, all animals need to live where they can survive. Now, let's learn about how they thrive in an ecosystem through their feeding habits.

Chapter 4: Producer-Consumer Relationships

At the beginning of this book, we learned about living things and their characteristics. In this final chapter, we will take a closer look at these living things, or organisms, and the three categories of jobs they are responsible for in the environment. We are going to learn about what these jobs are, how they interact with one another, and how important their relationships are to the ecosystem.

In an ecosystem, living organisms are also grouped by how they get food for energy. There are three main groups that have different jobs. Each group depends on the other for survival. The first are **producers**, which are plants that produce their own food through photosynthesis. The second are **consumers**, which need to eat other living things, such as plants or animals (or both), to get their energy. Finally, **decomposers** have the job of "recycling". They are living things that get their energy by breaking down dead plants, animals, and waste into smaller substances.

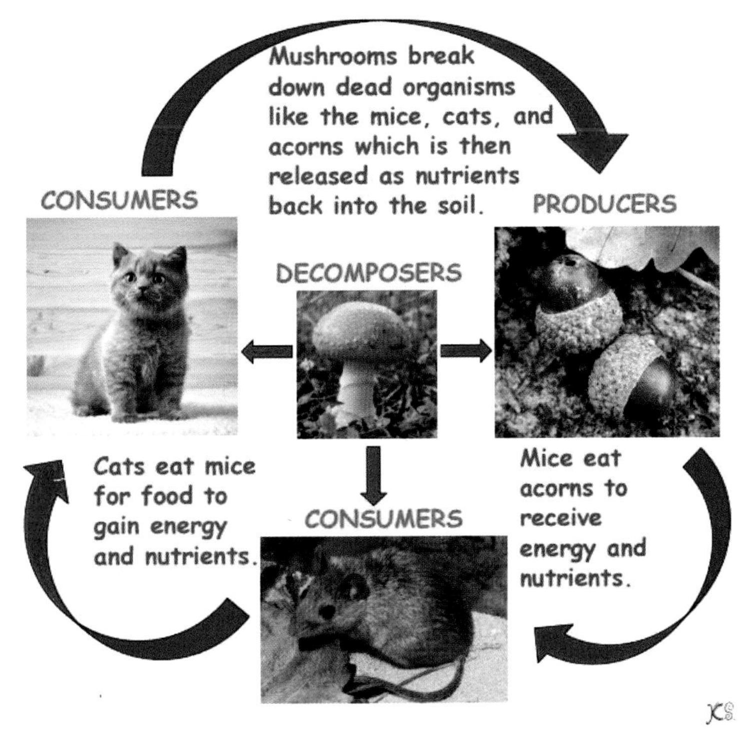

A **producer** is any green plant that makes its own food.

Producers: Plants and Produce

A **consumer** is an organism that cannot make its own food. It must eat producers or other consumers for energy. All animals are consumers.

Consumers: Animals consuming various parts of plants

Did you know? Many ecosystems have producers, primary consumers and secondary consumers. In the ocean for example, phytoplankton is a producer. Zooplankton, which are tiny animals, eat the plankton, and fish eat the zooplankton.

Consumers: Humans buying produce and flowers

Consumers: Humans eating and enjoying produce and flowers

A **decomposer** is an organism that gets energy by breaking down the remains of dead organisms. Decomposers are the last stop on the food chain. They can be referred to as nature's recyclers because they help keep nutrients moving in food webs. Their job is an important one, but is often overlooked. Decomposers are responsible for eating dead plants and animals, which help them break down into simpler substances. In the process, they release nutrients into the soil. If the decomposers did not do their job, the producers would not get the nutrients they need, and would die.

So what do these decomposers look like? Some of the most common decomposers are bacteria, worms, slugs, some insects, snails, and fungi like mushrooms. The earthworms in our backyards, the mushrooms in the forest, and all the clams in the ocean are also some examples of decomposers.

Decomposers: Earthworms, Mushrooms, and Clams

How Do Decomposers Work?

Decomposers eat dead things from the ground in order to get nutrients. The dead things that are eaten by decomposers are called detritus which means "garbage." They reduce dead animals, plants, and feces into chemicals. These chemicals become part of the soil, and the nutrients can then be used by living plants and the animals that consume them.

Decomposers in Different Ecosystems

Every ecosystem has different decomposers. Even though most decomposers cannot live in the Arctic, bacteria is one that can live there because it can live anywhere.

In the **forest** there are many different decomposers. Some of them are snails, slugs, earthworms, bacteria, and mushrooms. Whenever something dies in the forest, these are the decomposers that break the dead material down in order to provide nutrients for the soil.

Decomposers in the Forest: Mushrooms, Slug, and Snail

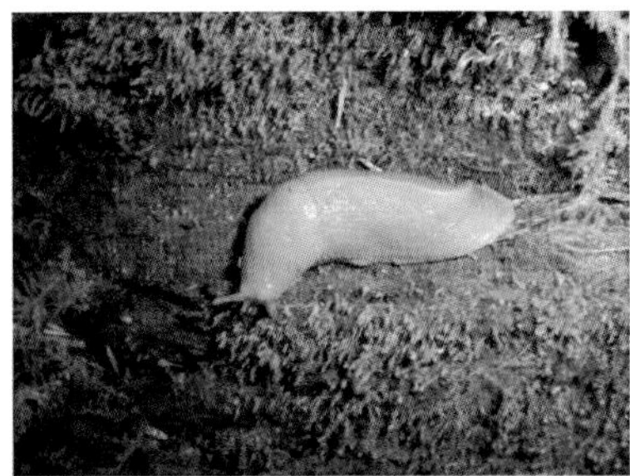

The **Desert** is a hard place for many decomposers to stay alive because they need to be in moist areas to survive. One of the only decomposers in the desert is bacteria because they are so small and can live in the air. Some of the other decomposers in the desert are beetles, earthworms and millipedes.

Decomposers in the Desert: Beetle, Earthworm, and Millipedes

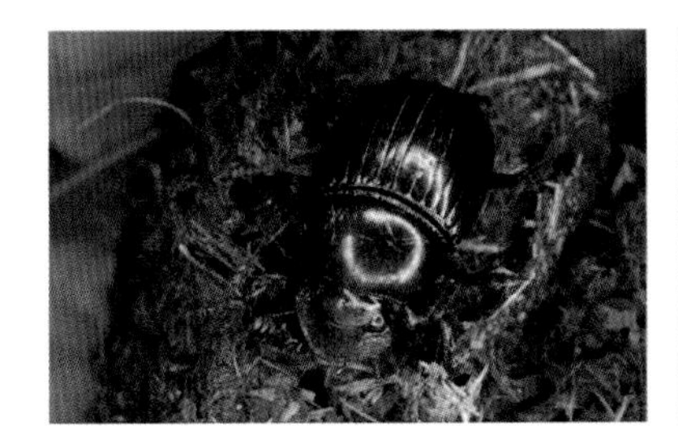

There are not many types of decomposers in the **water**. Most types of decomposers in the water are different types of bacteria. S**cavengers** such as freshwater shrimp, clams, crabs, lobsters, and flatworms also feed on the bodies of dead animals and plants in the water.

Decomposers in the Water: Bacteria filled water, clams, and freshwater shrimp

Decomposers: Different Types of Bacteria Viewed Under a Microscope

 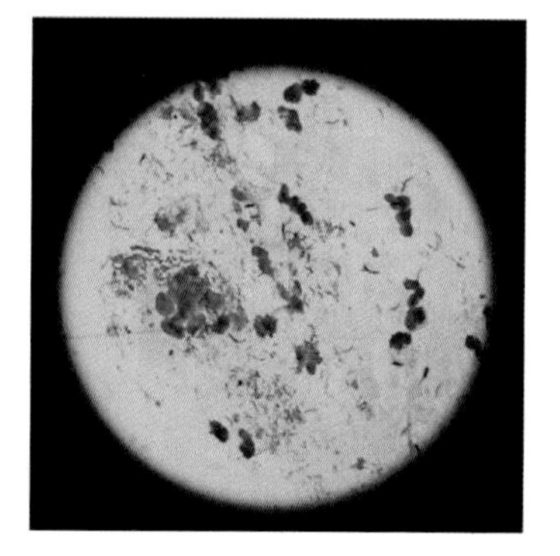 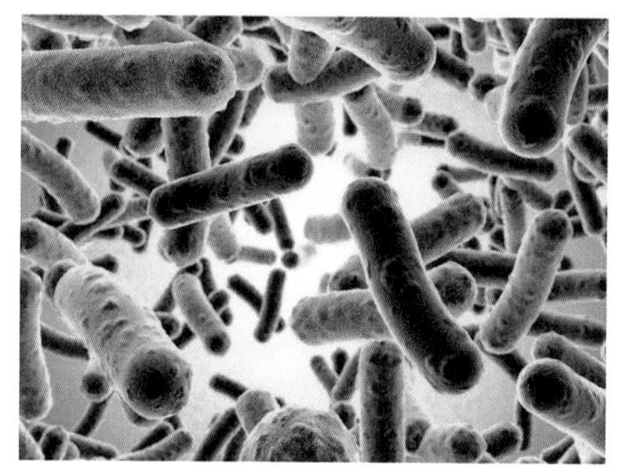

Did you know? Some decomposers, like snails and worms, can also be consumers because they eat plants too.

Food Chains

All living things depend on other living things for food. A **food chain** is a natural order of what eats what. A living thing must consume something for energy and survival. Animals cannot make their own food, so they eat plants and other animals, and are called **Consumers**. Plants make their own food and are called **Producers**.

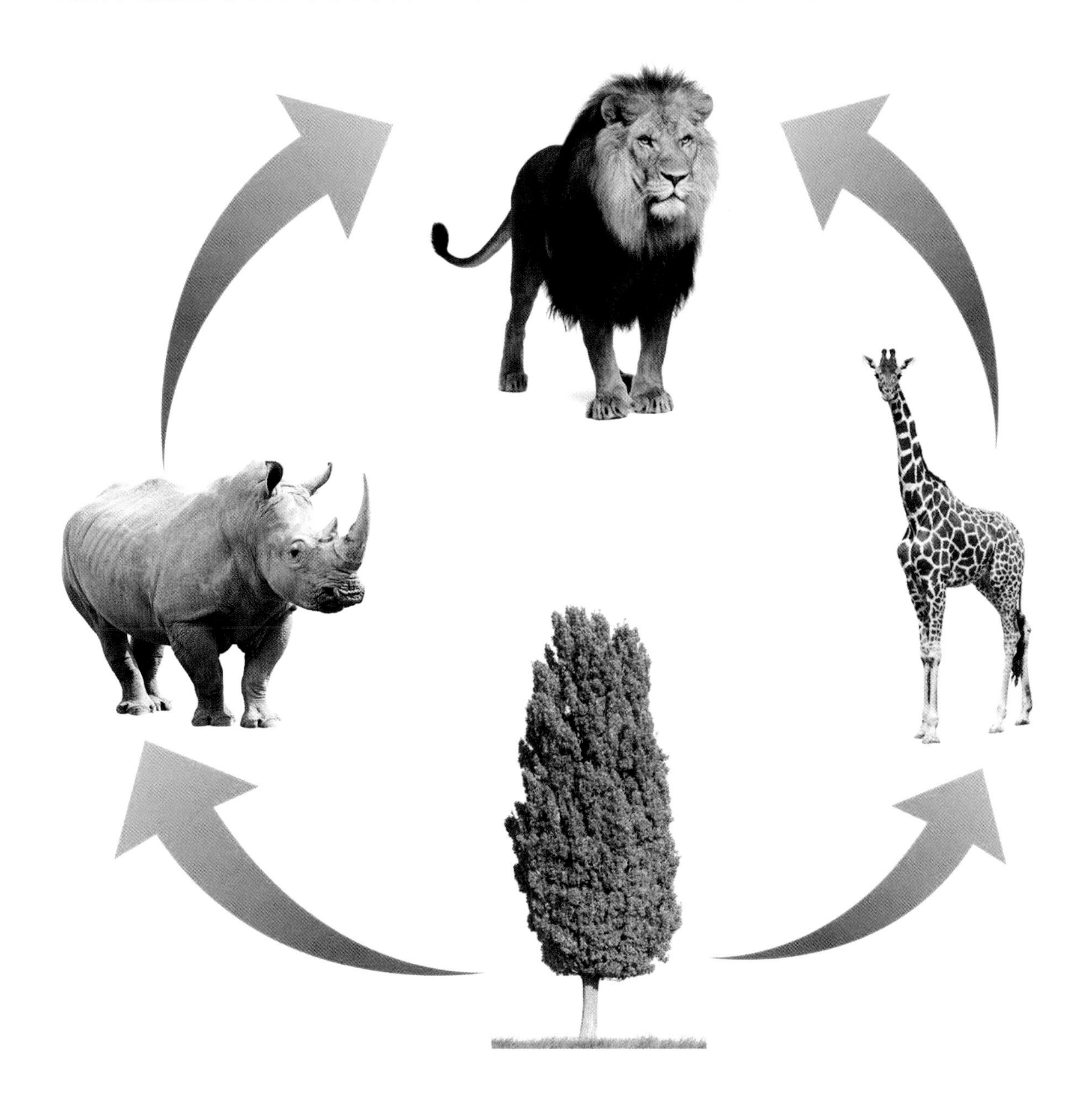

Examples of Food Chains

At the beginning of a food chain, you will find smaller organisms fed upon by a larger one, which in turn feeds a still larger one, etc. Humans are somewhere at the end of the food chain.

Caterpillars eat leaves ⇨ birds eat caterpillars ⇨ cats eat birds

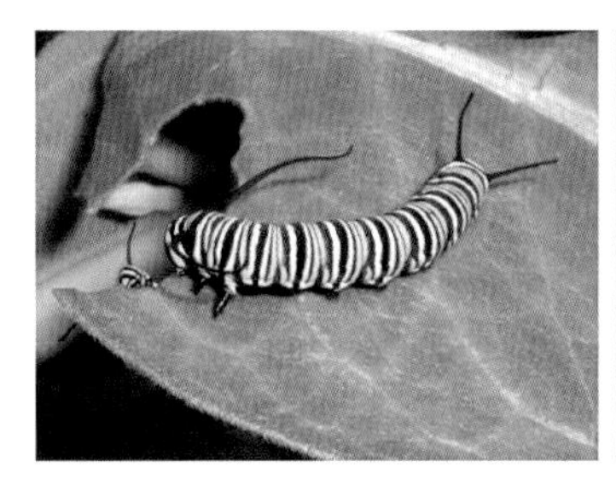

Bees eat nectar ⇨ birds eat bees ⇨ squirrels eat birds

Mice eat corn ⇨ owls eat mice ⇨ foxes eat owls

Small fish eat algae ➪ medium and big fish eat smaller fish

Fish eat seaweeds ➪ seals eat fish ➪ polar bears eat seals

Zebras eats grass ➪ leopards eats zebras

Food Pyramid

The **food pyramid** on the next page shows how living things get food and energy, and recycle nutrients. The bottom row consists of **primary producers**, which are green plants that make their own food through photosynthesis. They are a source of energy for the organisms that eat them. The row above are **primary consumers** such as caterpillars and rabbits that consume only plants. **Secondary consumers** such as foxes and raccoons, make up the next row above that. These types of consumers are omnivores and carnivores. They get their energy from food sources that belong to the bottom two categories.

Tertiary consumers are at the top of the pyramid. Examples include carnivores like lions and snakes. When these organisms on all levels die, **decomposers** break them down and extract the last bit of energy from them and convert them into nutrients for the soil. Primary producers then take in these nutrients through the soil, and the cycle continues.

Which group does each of the living things below belong to?

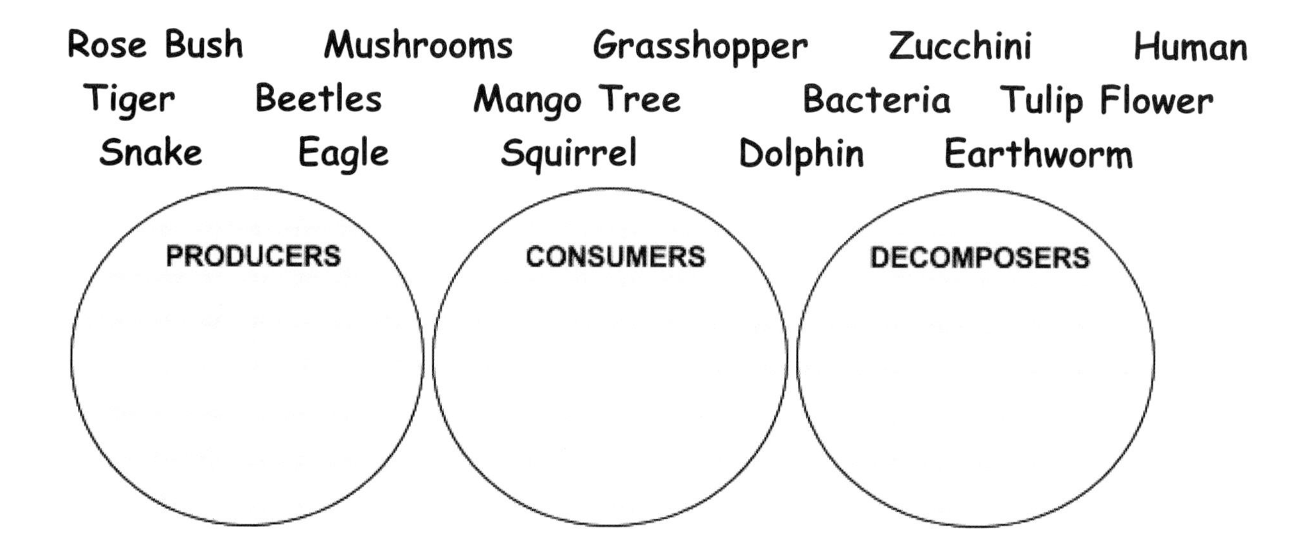

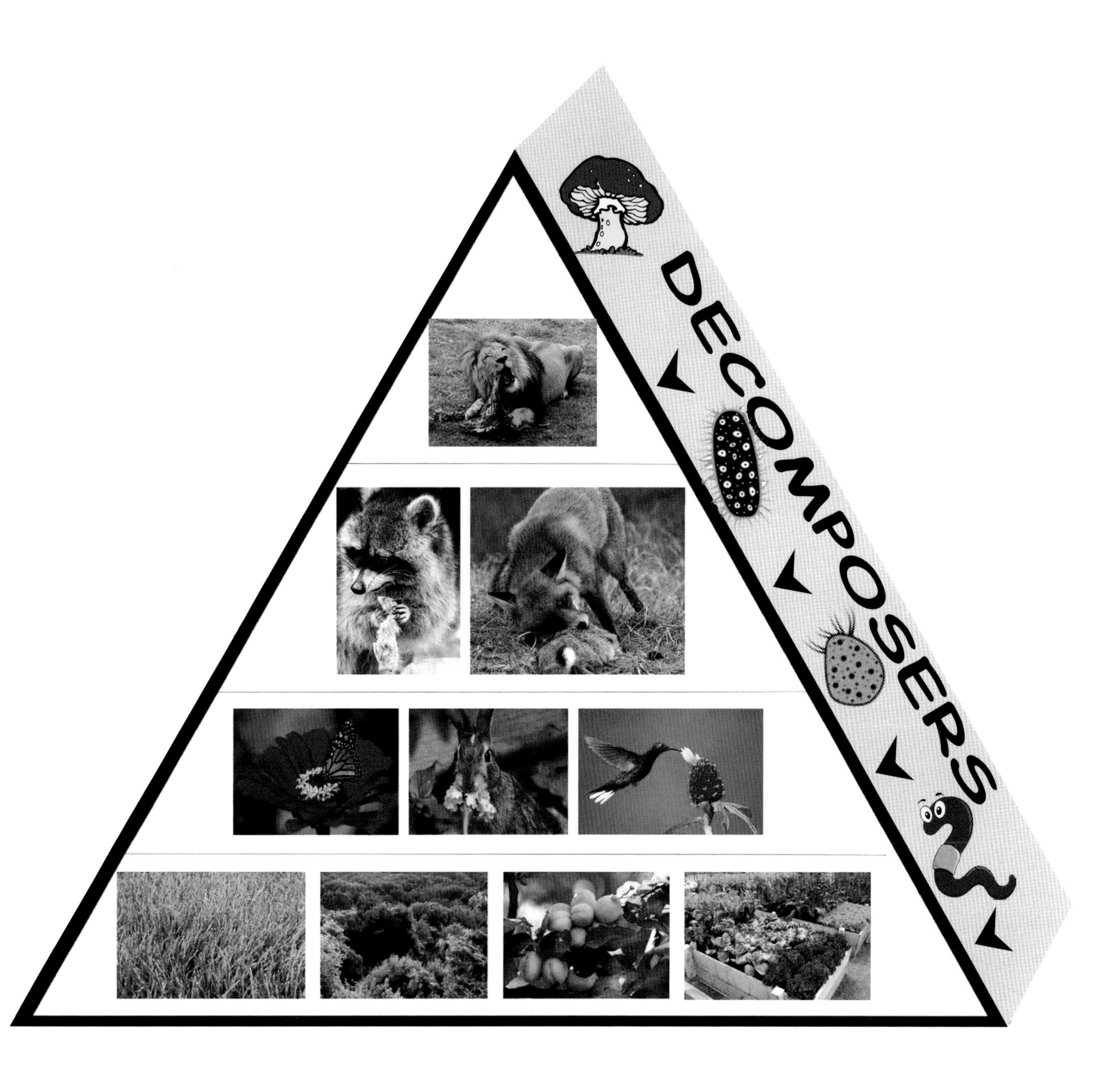
DECOMPOSERS

Our Planet

We have learned about the many living and nonliving things that exist on our planet. As humans, we depend on so many things to survive and thrive. Let us learn to respect and take care of our environment, so we can all survive together in harmony.

About the Authors

Vidya Sudarsan is an engineer by profession. 8 years ago, she ended her successful career in Silicon Valley to devote more time to her family and focus on her children's growing needs. She is a proud mother of two teenaged daughters, the older of whom is a college sophomore. Her younger daughter, a homeschooler on the autism spectrum, served as the inspiration and motivation for creating this book.

Sarah Jane Edward-Sebeni is an entrepreneur with a background in education, applied linguistics, and TESOL. She scaled back from a thriving business in academic tutoring to concentrate on her family. She is a busy mom of three school aged daughters.

The two are friends with common interests and are passionate advocates for children with learning challenges particularly within the ASD (autism) and ADHD communities. Together, they started their company, EdVisually, with a vision to promote awareness and create tools for visual learners. It is their hope to bring the joy of learning to visual and special needs learners in classrooms around the world.

Credits

Content Consultants:
Pamela Emeahara -Science Teacher, St. Elizabeth Elementary, Oakland CA
Neha Prabhu -Highschool Student

Content Reviewers:
Jennifer Adams Oppenheimer, MA, CCC-SLP -Speech-Language Pathologist, Founder, SpeakJoy Center for Development

Teacher Reviewers:
Pamela Emeahara -Science Teacher, St. Elizabeth Elementary, Oakland CA
Lisa Hillman -Special Ed Teacher, Glankler Preschool, Fremont, CA
Vathsala Sridharan -Nursery Teachers Educator, Delhi, India

Design Credits:
Cover Design -Vidya Sudarsan & Sarah Jane Edward-Sebeni

Illustration Credits:
14: "Parts of a Plant" -Kesiena Sebeni; 43: "Life Cycle of a Plant" -Kesiena Sebeni; 44: "Photosynthesis in Plants" -Kesiena Sebeni; 48: "Animal Senses" -Encyclopedia Britannica, Inc.; 61: "Butterfly & Grasshopper Life Cycle"- biology-forums.com/index.php?action=gallery;sa=view;id=922; 77: "Producer-Consumer-Decomposer Cycle" -Kesiena Sebeni

Photo Credits (t = top; b = bottom; c = center; l = left; r = right):
Individual Contributors: 59 (tl) Shark by K. A. Jagannathan; 70 (tl) Three Sisters by Liliana Muntean
Istockphoto by Getty Images: 4: (l) BeholdingEye; 5: (b) Christopher Futcher; 6-7: all, 8-9: all, 10: (c) Benjamin Howell; 11: (tl, cl, cr, br), (bl) Ajay Kampani; 13: all, 17: all, 20: (l, c, r), 21: (l, c, r), 22: (c), 23: (tl), 24-25: all, 26: all, 28: all, 29: (tr)Tutye, 30: (tc, cc), 32: all, 37: all, 40: all, 42: (all), 43: (bc); 46: (bl) Oksana Zahray; 46: (bc) Christopher Futcher; 46: (br) svetikd; 48-49: all except 49: (br) monkeybusinessimages; 50: all, (tr) Steve Davenport; 51: (tr) Steve Debenport;, 52: all, 53: all; 55: (t,b), 62: (tl, tc, tr); 66: (t) Christopher Futcher; 66: (bl) TriggerPhoto; 66: (br), 67: (tl) Miroslav Ferkuniak; 67: (tr) Seth_Haussler_Photograph; 67: (cr) JackQ; 67: (bl) vm; 67: (br) simonkr; 68: (t1) Susan Chiang; 68: (t3) vgajic; 69: (tl) Mordolff; 69: (tr) AlexRaths; 69: (cl) kynesher; 69: (br) Cristian Lazzari; 70: (bl) monkeybusinessimages ; 70: (br) Vikram Raghuvanshi; 73: all, 74-75: all, 76: all, 80: (tl) Steve Debenport; 80: (cl)Dmitry Kalinovsky; 80: (bl) Lady buying flowers: Steve Debenport; 80: (tr) James Tutor; 81: (tl) filo; 81: (tc)kolinko_tanya; 81: (tr) Birgitte Magnus; 81: (cr) junce; 84: (bl, bc, br), 85: all, 90: (c); **Shutterstock:** 11: (tr) Ruth Black; 14: (br) Serhiy Kobyakov; 44: (c) logoboom; 56: (ctr) Delmas Lehman; 57: (br) Cathy Keifer;
Freeimages.com: 15: (tl) myrtle-1621312 -Patrizio Martorana; (tc) oranges-1326939 -Onur Mumcu; (tr) pomegranate-1-1509147 -Alex Ringer; (bl) apple-1327789 -Onur Mumcu; (bc) papaya-srb-1321067-Sergio Roberto Bichara; (br) grapes-1562231 -J. Gabriel; 16: (l)

vine-flowers-1343638 -Hilda Joyce; (ct) flower-1354190 -Wojtek Hintzke; (cb) sunflower-1366211 -Foreverkid; (r) rose-1378451 -Sorina Bindea; (bl) flowers-1443118 - Roger Kirby; (bc) vase-1465563 - Diane Miller; (br)flowers-1630368 -Michael & Christa Richert; 41: (tr) daisies-1393484 -jdkoenig; (bl) strawberry-1322093 - sm jet; (br) foliage-1408734 -Palmer W.Cook; (b) zinnia-1146929 -Fran Liden; 29: (bl) donkey-1543623 -Joanna Atkinson; (br) horse-1392891 -Mef Felles; 30: (bl) rabbit-1355714 -Maple Rose; 31: (bc) dog-1408147 -Niklas Steffen; 31: (br) lion-1346240 -Sergio Venturi; 45: (all) seagull-4-1245201 -Miguel Saavedra; wild-boar-1336864 -Andreas Krappweis; lamb-1396615 -Anthony Robson; lounging-snake-1548754 -Jeffrey Collingwood; squirrel-monkey-1572877 -Marieke Kuijpers; butterfly-1389754 -John Boyer; dolphin-2-1372853 -Stacy Brumley; tree-frog-1353116 -Nate Brelsford; jaguar-1310184 -Martin M Hernandez Tena; 53: (tl) frog-2-1342397 -Sias van Schalkwy; (tc)frog-1551325 -Bill Sarver; (tr)frog-1246663 -Michel Meynsbrughen; 55: (tc) 124687285 -Khoroshunova Olga; (tb) turtle-1367849 -Izabelha; 56: (bl) snake-1569213 -Saivann; (bc) snake-1469469 -Kenn Kiser; (bb)snake-1534134 -yoann yoann; 57: (bl) green-lizard-1400251 -Louise Jensen; 58 (tl) fish-1176775 -Thad Zajdowicz; (tc) pisces-1545637 -Griszka Niewiadomski; (tr) fish-1507444 -Roma Rishkin; 60: (b1) ladybug-1393193 -Angela Gunder; (b2) mouche-04-1497483 -Alex Drahon; (b3) spider-1461175 -Sylke P.; (b4) damselfly-1539302 -Wojciech Doros; (b5) grasshopper-1-1371229 -Elivs Santana; 62: (b1) robin's eggs-1369170 -Karen Barefoot; (b2) egret-1398659 -Kalyana Sundaram; (b3) hummingbird nest-1387547 -René Madariaga; (b1) bird-1404694 -Magda S.; (b2) duck-1470363 -Sreekanth Devarajan; (b3) toucan-1504489 -Rogério Medeiros Pinho; (b4) blue-jay-1377788 -Jeff Jones; **Other Websites:** Images are licensed under a Creative Commons Attribution-ShareAlike 4.0 International License. theonebaja.com: 4 (r) Killer Whale; clintonchaloner.co.uk/images/galleries/fallenoak/fallenoak.html: 14 (bl) Xylem; vincentkohler.ch/billon.html: 23 (cl) Billon -Geoffrey Cottonceau; animals.nationalgeographic.com: 27 Chimp -Michel Nichols; en.wikipedia.org: 27 Koala -JJ Harrison; zooblog.ru: 27 Bears; community.qvc.com: 27 Bird's Nest -Tissyanne; nationalgeographic.com: 34 animals-resting-on-trees; epod.typepad.com: 35 (b); iltwmt.com: 36; flickr.com/photos/cochrun/5655042858: 57 (t) alligator -Cochrun; content.ces.ncsu.edu/extension-gardener-handbook/4-insects: 60 (t) Insect Parts; kids.nationalgeographic.com/animals/flamingo/#flamingo-group.jpg: 63 (tr) Flamingos; voices.nationalgeographic.com/2012/03/23/top-25-wild-bird-photographs-of-the-week-7-4/swallow-tailed-bee-eaters-sitting-together-in-the-morning-sun-michele-nel/: 63 (tl) green birds -Michele Nel; pixabay.com/en/family-toddler-love-mom-dad-kiss-1244795/: 66 (br) mom, dad, baby -AdinaVoicu; tlc.com/tv-shows/cake-boss/: 69 (bl); dreamstime.com: 29 (bc) cow, 79: (tc) cow, (cl) panda 79: (tl) bunny 79: (br) hummington;

Resources

Books:

California Science. Macmillan/McGraw-Hill, 2008.
Encyclopedia of Science. DK Publishing, 2006.

Websites:

www.animals.nationalgeographic.com; kids.nationalgeographic.com; en.wikipedia.org; www.eol.org; www.msnucleus.org; www.biology.tutorvista.com; www.ducksters.com; www.kids.britannica.com; www.study.com; www.easyscienceforkids.com; wls.k12.oh.us; www.dkfindout.com/us

Index

(p= photo, i= illustration)

Watch out for some of our other upcoming Science Visually books!

- Physical Science
- Human Body
- Space